Torque: Clarity On The US Waterboarding Policy Is Necessary To Combat Impunity

AN INTRODUCTION TO THE ISSUES

Kaitlin Puccio

Bent Frame Publishing | New York, NY

Copyright © 2020 by Kaitlin Puccio.

All rights reserved. No part of this publication may be reproduced, distributed, or transmitted in any form or by any means, including photocopying, recording, or other electronic or mechanical methods, without the prior written permission of the Publisher, except in the case of brief quotations embodied in critical reviews and certain other noncommercial uses permitted by copyright law.

www.bentframepublishing.com
www.kayelabs.com

Torque: Clarity On The US Waterboarding Policy Is Necessary To Combat Impunity/ Kaitlin Puccio.
ISBN 978-0-9964329-7-9
Library of Congress Control Number: 2020952301

Contents

Introduction 1

Background: What is torture, legally? 4

Analysis: Waterboarding as a case study 8

Conclusion 40

A Special Topics Publication for
Celia Kaye | Kaye Labs

CeliaKaye

[1]

INTRODUCTION

IN THE YEARS following the September 11, 2001 terrorist attacks, the debate over torture largely came to take place within the context of waterboarding. Nearly two decades after the attacks, there remains no consensus about what precisely constitutes torture, whether waterboarding fits any of the currently existing definitions of torture, and whether torture is permissible in certain instances. Such confusion may result in impunity for interrogators, a perception of US weakness in the eyes of the international community, or a suspicion that because the US is secretive about its waterboarding practices it must be committing other atrocities as well.

The torture debate in the United States has three parts. First, the legal debate: What is the legal definition of torture? Second, the pragmatic debate: Does torture work? Third, the moral debate: Is torture ever morally permissible in order to obtain the information needed to save lives? I will analyze the three parts of the torture debate largely in the context of waterboarding. I will first argue that waterboarding does not fit the legal definition of torture. Next I will argue that torture generally works, even if it results in some instances of misleading information. Then I will examine the morality of torture, addressing whether the definition of torture must be expanded to encompass waterboarding, whether the necessity defense is valid from deontological and utilitarian ethics perspectives, and the moral implications of using information gathered as a result of potentially unethical acts. I will then propose a practical solution to the debate given the need for clarity to protect against impunity, highlighted by a recently settled case against two psychologists who helped develop the Central Intelligence Agency's post-9/11 interrogation program. Finally, I conclude that even if waterboarding is legally not torture and is morally permissible in certain situations, it may nevertheless be necessary to stipulate that waterboarding is impermissible as a policy matter, because the information gained through waterboarding may not outweigh the information lost when nations are no longer willing to share intelligence with the US because we are seen as a nation that tortures.

[2]

BACKGROUND: WHAT IS TORTURE, LEGALLY?

THERE IS NO universally accepted definition of torture, though there are some common elements among the various definitions. The agreed upon elements that make up torture are that it is 1) an act, 2) that is intentional, 3) which causes severe mental or physical pain or suffering. The Convention against Torture and Other Cruel, Inhuman or Degrading Treatment or Punishment (CAT) defines torture in Article 1:

> ...[T]orture means any act by which severe pain or suffering, whether physical or mental, is intentionally inflicted on a person for such purposes as obtaining from him or a third person information

> *or a confession, punishing him for an act he or a third person has committed or is suspected of having committed, or intimidating or coercing him or a third person, or for any reason based on discrimination of any kind, when such pain or suffering is inflicted by or at the instigation of or with the consent or acquiescence of a public official or other person acting in an official capacity.*[1]

The Rome Statute of the International Criminal Court defines torture similarly:

> *'Torture' means the intentional infliction of severe pain or suffering, whether physical or mental, upon a person in the custody or under the control of the accused...*[2]

Finally, 18 U.S. Code § 2441 points to similar elements found in the above two definitions of torture:

> *The act of a person who commits, or conspires or attempts to commit, an act specifically intended to inflict severe physical or mental pain or suffering...upon another person within his custody or physical control for the purpose of obtaining information or a confession, punishment, intimidation, coercion, or any reason based on discrimination of any kind.*[3]

CAT and 18 U.S. Code § 2441 agree that such an act is committed for the purpose of obtaining information. The Rome Statute and 18 U.S. Code § 2441 agree that the act must be committed upon a person in custody or within the physical control of the accused torturer. The first two of the three agreed upon elements of torture—an "act" that is "intentional"—are largely uncontested as applied to waterboarding.[4] An interrogator intentionally implements the technique of waterboarding during an interrogation. Whether waterboarding "causes severe mental or physical pain or suffering" is less clear, and will be addressed in part III.A.2.

A single, clear definition of torture that balances the need for information while deterring abuse is aspirational. Clarity would lead to accountability rather than impunity when interrogators cross into the realm of torture (which under CAT would require them to be criminally prosecuted) from the realm of cruel, inhuman, or degrading treatment or punishment (CIDTP) that falls short of torture. Because it is unlikely that there will ever be an agreed upon, correct definition of torture given the numerous perspectives that would be involved in an attempt to craft such a definition, it is necessary instead to determine if waterboarding ought to be permissible, whether or not it legally constitutes torture.

[3]

ANALYSIS: WATERBOARDING AS A CASE STUDY

A. Waterboarding does not fit the legal definitions of torture

1. Mechanism and physiology of waterboarding

NPR DESCRIBES WATERBOARDING as a "simulated drowning technique"[5] involving a subject who lies on his back immobilized on a declined platform. A cloth is placed over his nose and mouth, and water is poured intermittently onto the cloth and enters the breathing passages. The intended effect of waterboarding an individual is not to drown him, but to make him feel like he is drowning. A drowned individual is indicative of waterboarding gone wrong. How does waterboarding induce the sensation of drowning without actually drowning an individual?

According to Coral Dando, Professor of Psychology at the University of Westminster, London, the inhalation of water causes a gag reflex. The individual experiences "what amounts to drowning as their body assumes that death is imminent."[6] In essence, the individual's mind betrays his body. He feels like he is being asphyxiated. However, due to the declined position of the individual which elevates his lungs above his head and neck, his lungs do not fill with water, which would be a necessary element of drowning. Most of the water remains in the individual's nasal cavity, and though some water may indeed enter the lungs in some instances, the individual is not asphyxiated. Thus, there is a necessary step in between the act of the interrogator and the harm caused in order for waterboarding to be effective: the gag reflex. The act of waterboarding is an indirect cause of an avoidable harm.

2. Waterboarding is, legally, neither mental nor physical torture

It may be argued that waterboarding causes mental harm rather than physical, given that a subject *feels* like he is being asphyxiated. Psychological torture, in comparison with physical torture, can be thought of as breaking the mind rather than breaking bones by stressing a victim's "conditions for mental survival."[7] These conditions are referred to by psychologists as homeostasis, where an individual makes adjustments in order to maintain internal equilibrium despite changes to external stimuli. Psychological torture disrupts a victim's homeostasis by overwhelming the victim's ability to make the necessary adjustments to extreme external stimuli.

The 1994 Convention against Torture lists four pathways by which an act constitutes torture: 1) the intentional infliction or threatened infliction of severe physical pain or suffering; 2) the administration or application, or threatened administration or application, of mind-altering substances or other procedures calculated to disrupt profoundly the senses or the personality; 3) the threat of imminent death; 4) or the threat that another person will be subjected to any of these.[8]

The waterboarding analysis is concerned with 2) and 3).

The Defense Department Working Group Report on Detainee Interrogations in the Global War on Terrorism ("Report") states that mock executions are considered psychological torture because the victim is made to believe that his death is imminent.[9] Imminence requires that the threat be immediate and certain. The immediacy requirement speaks to "conditions for mental survival" because the victim's homeostasis is disrupted by the stress of imminent death, and he does not have time to make adjustments to maintain equilibrium. By contrast, the Report specifies that a "vague threat that someday [he] might be killed" does not satisfy the immediacy requirement, and therefore does not constitute mental pain or suffering.[10] An individual who is told that he is about to be waterboarded is less likely to believe that his death is imminent than an individual who is told that he is about to be executed. Waterboarding is unlike an execution because the intended end is not to kill, but to extract information.

There are other categories of psychological torture in which waterboarding potentially fits. The Report lists "the administration or application or threatened administration or application of mind-altering substances or other procedures calculated to disrupt profoundly the senses or the personality."[11] While waterboarding is not a mind-altering substance, it must be considered whether it is "[an]other procedure calculated to disrupt profoundly the senses." The Report interprets "disrupt" as meaning "to break asunder; to part forcibly." The technique of waterboarding relies on an individual's senses—his gag reflex—to be working properly. Indeed, if his gag reflex were disrupted or broken, he would not feel the sensation of drowning. Therefore, waterboarding is not a procedure calculated to "disrupt profoundly" the senses, but a procedure predicated on the good working condition of the senses throughout the interrogation.

If waterboarding is not mental torture, perhaps it is physical torture.[12] Physical torture has been pervasive throughout history. The Tang Dynasty introduced death by a thousand cuts.[13] This form of torture—known as lingchi—was used until 1905. The torturer would deliver a series of cuts to a rulebreaker's skin, first removing small pieces of tissue and muscle, then continuing on to another area. The smaller each incision, the longer it took for the victim to die, which allowed the executioner to prolong the suffering of his victim before death.

Unlike lingchi, which was used as punishment, the torture methods used during the Spanish Inquisition were employed to extract confessions.[14] Possibly the most famous of these devices is the rack, where a victim lies on a rectangular wooden frame with rollers on either end. His ankles are bound to one end and his wrists are bound above his head to the other. The inquisitor would turn a crank attached to the rollers, which would increase the tension on the ropes as the victim's limbs were slowly pulled away from his body. Often this led to dislocated joints and permanent disfigurement, but the rack could be operated with such enthusiasm that it would rip a victim's limbs off completely. The inquisitor often forced others to watch this process in an effort to demonstrate what would happen to them if they did not confess.

Physical torture is still used today. In 2017, Human Rights Watch reported that Egypt routinely subjects victims to electric shocks while being held in stress positions and beaten. One of those stress positions is the strappado, where a victim's arms are raised backward behind him and suspended by some form of rope attached to his wrists. This typically results in dislocated shoulders—a technique that dates back to the Spanish Inquisition.[15]

These techniques, all of which fit the current definition of torture, share one key element: the proximity of the act to the resulting harm. In all instances, there is an act that directly causes a severe and unavoidable harm. For example, the rack illustrates an act that directly results in an unavoidable harm. The turning of the crank results in the dislocation of the joints. In order to understand how the proximity of the act to the harm in waterboarding distinguishes it from these torture techniques, it is necessary to revisit the mechanism.

In the case of waterboarding, there is a critical step in between the act of the interrogator and the resulting harm: Waterboarding relies on the subject's gag reflex to kick in. The technique would fail without this step. If the subject's gag reflex were suppressed or otherwise non-functional, the harm would not result from the act. The harm—the sensation of asphyxiation—is an avoidable harm, unlike the harm that results from the inquisitor's turning of the crank. This extra factor necessary to the infliction of harm is what makes waterboarding fall outside the scope of the definition of torture—it is the step after the act—the gag reflex—that results in "serious physical or mental pain or suffering."

The definition does not specify that the act must *directly* result in harm to be torture. This can be inferred, however, by using what the definition says that torture is not. The Convention against Torture and Other Cruel, Inhuman or Degrading Treatment or Punishment states that "[Torture] does not include pain or suffering arising only from, inherent in or *incidental to* lawful sanctions."[16] By including the italicized language, the drafters were clearly aware of the concept of incidental consequences in the context of lawful sanctions. It can be deduced that because incidental harm is not included in the definition of torture, it was deliberately left out. Assuming that this existing definition of torture is correct, waterboarding falls outside the scope of this definition because the harm inflicted is incidental to the act. In other words, the act indirectly—or incidentally—results in the subject's suffering if the subject's gag reflex, which is the direct cause of the suffering, is not subdued. No harm would come about but for the fact that the subject has a physiological response to the water.

Torture is at its core, a tort.[17] Indeed, the word "torture" would not exist without, first, "tort." The two words share the common Latin root "torquere," meaning "to twist." A tort is an act or omission that gives rise to injury or harm to another.[18] Intentional torts result from an intentional act.[19] An intentional tort shares many elements with the definition of torture in that it must 1) be an act or omission, 2) be intentional, and 3) result in harm. Torture raises the stakes and demands that this harm be severe. If torture can be thought of as an extreme tort, tort law—in a simplified form—can help clarify the "actual cause" requirement. The relationship between the act or omission and the harm is a chain. If there are any intervening links, the chain is broken, and the act is not said to be the actual (or "but-for") cause of the harm.[20] In the case of waterboarding, if a subject is able to suppress his gag reflex, he will not feel like he is drowning. That is, but for a functioning gag reflex, no harm or suffering would result from waterboarding. Thus, the act of waterboarding would not be said to be the actual cause of the harm, and would not constitute physical torture.

B. Torture works

If torture did not work, there would be a strong moral argument against it. However, as argued below, torture does work. That does not necessarily mean, however, that other methods are not as effective as torture. It may be argued that torture does not work because it may at times result in false confessions, misinformation, or incomplete truths—or that information gathered that has been attributed to torture was really gathered as a result of "rapport-building." While this is true in some cases, interrogators do not rely solely on the information gained from single individuals before taking action.[21] The information gathered is checked against and viewed in light of information gathered from other detainees as well as other sources of intelligence to verify its validity. Disclosures made by victims of torturous interrogations at the hands of the CIA were critical to the discovery of the location of Osama bin Laden's hideout in Pakistan.[22] The CIA, through an intelligence cross-checking (or "connect-the-dots") strategy, was able to identify and follow bin Laden's courier, Ahmed the Kuwaiti, who carried messages between bin Laden in his compound and al Qaeda. A Navy SEAL team was subsequently able to eliminate bin Laden, who was responsible for the September 11, 2001 attacks in the US and the decade of terror that followed, during which ordinary life for many Americans changed.

Given the strategy of piecing together information extracted via interrogations, even if single interrogation sessions do not yield a complete truth, they are not meant to; the information obtained is one data point considered alongside other data points to check for veracity as well as to make useful information connections.[23]

However, this does not necessarily mean that torture works in all or most instances, or that it is the only means of effectively extracting information. According to the Senate Select Committee on Intelligence Study of the CIA's Detention and Interrogation Program, FBI agents used non-coercive rapport-building techniques in their interrogations of detainee Abu Zubaydah, who was cooperative.[24] The CIA claimed, rather, that the intelligence gathered resulted from torture rather than rapport-building.[25] While it may not be possible to know exactly what happened, or what it was that worked, citing specific instances in a vacuum of when torture works and when rapport-building works means little.

Given our ethical inability to conduct research to study how effective torture is versus non-coercive methods of information gathering, the best option may be to consult psychologists for their expert opinion on the most effective techniques for extracting information from a resistant individual. As discussed in section C. below, the CIA did in fact consult with psychologists on this matter, but the results were not as expected.

C. The morality of torture

If waterboarding fits within a subcategory of acts that would be considered torture but for the fact that they are one step removed from being the actual cause of the severe mental or physical harm or suffering, perhaps there is no correct definition of torture in existence. If we accept that there is a plausible argument that waterboarding does not constitute legal torture, perhaps the correct definition of torture needs to be modified so that waterboarding is classified as torture. One argument against expanding the definition of torture to encompass waterboarding is that waterboarding is necessary in the interest of national security. In *US v. Oakland Cannabis Buyers*,[26] the Supreme Court addresses whether there is a necessity defense in federal law, stating that "it is an open question whether federal courts ever have authority to recognize a necessity defense not provided by statute." Thus, international cases may provide guidance.

In the 1976 case *Ireland v. United Kingdom*,[27] the European Commission of Human Rights considered whether the interrogation methods used by British authorities in 1971 on fourteen Northern Irish persons questioning their involvement with the Irish Republican Army during "the longest and most violent terrorist campaign witnessed in either part of the island of Ireland" amounted to torture.[28]

The five interrogation techniques used in 1971 included wall standing, hooding, subjection to continuous and loud noise, sleep deprivation, and deprivation of food and drink.[29] Responding to several allegations of ill-treatment that year, the UK established the Compton Committee to investigate.[30] The Committee justified the use of the techniques, stating that they were used to interrogate persons who were "believed to possess information of a kind which it was operationally necessary to obtain as rapidly as possible in the interest of saving lives."[31]

After the Compton Committee's findings were met with criticism, the UK appointed the Parker Committee. The Parker Committee was tasked with determining "whether, and if so in what respects, the procedures currently authorized for the interrogation of persons suspected of terrorism and for their custody while subject to interrogation require amendment."[32] A majority and a minority report were submitted in 1972. The minority report maintained that the techniques were not morally justifiable, "even in the light of any marginal advantages which might have been obtained."[33] The majority report asserted that the morality depended on the intensity with which the techniques were applied, and the existence of safeguards against their excessive use.[34]

In *Public Committee Against Torture in Israel v. State of Israel*,[35] the petitioner, who was part of a terrorist group, was arrested and interrogated by General Security Service (GSS) investigators in Israel. The petitioner alleged that he was tortured, claiming that he was deprived of sleep and was subject to the "Shabach" stress position. The court in *Israel* recognized a necessity defense available to an interrogator who faces criminal charges for cruel physical treatment (but not torture) of a criminal suspect. The interrogator may assert the necessity defense where gaining information quickly is necessary to save lives. The court further posits that in such cases, "society is choosing the lesser evil. Not only is it legitimately permitted to engage in fighting terrorism, it is our moral duty to employ the means necessary for this purpose."[36]

The decisions are important to show that the necessity defense is legitimate in international law, and also to show how easily such a defense can lead to impunity. For example, if an interrogator knows that waterboarding may or may not be a criminal act, where the necessity defense is available he is more likely to apply the technique than he would be if there were no necessity defense, which would likely render him more apt to proceed with caution. One "safeguard" against this type of excessive use, as the Parker majority wrote, is to more clearly delineate whether waterboarding is torture. If waterboarding is not torture, then under Israel, interrogators may avail themselves of the necessity defense. Where there is vagueness, as there is currently, the interrogator cannot be said to have notice that his actions are criminal, and therefore he cannot be held liable.

Where the US is entrenched in a "war on terror," the legitimacy of the necessity defense is a critical issue. The September 11, 2001 attacks made it clear that terrorists' threats are not hollow, and terrorism remains an issue. FBI Director Christopher Wray has stated that today's terrorism threats come from al Qaeda as well as other terror groups, sleeper cells, and domestic terrorists.[37] Daniel Coats, Director of National Intelligence, has stated that al Qaeda "remains intent on attacking the United States and U.S. interests abroad."[38] In light of this, it would be easy to accept the necessity defense as valid in the interest of national security.

However, accepting the necessity defense requires an ethical analysis. There are two schools of ethics that directly conflict with each other when analyzing the validity of the defense: utilitarianism and deontology. Utilitarianism is the view that the morally correct action is that which produces the greatest good for the greatest number.[39] By contrast, deontology is the view that the morality of an action is based on whether the action itself is ethical.[40] A deontologist would consider whether waterboarding is ethical in itself without considering the consequences.

Imagine that the CIA has a known terrorist, X, in custody, and urgently needs information from him in order to save American lives.[41] A utilitarian would argue that a pressing need for information would justify the use of waterboarding as a means of interrogation because the purpose is to extract information that would save the lives of many. A deontologist would argue that waterboarding X is not justified because the act itself is unethical, therefore it does not matter on whom the act is imposed or whether the act was done with the intention of saving thousands of lives. A deontologist would essentially distill the analysis and determine that X is a person, it is wrong to waterboard people, therefore it is wrong to waterboard X.

There is an obligation to respond to the needs of the public and to act reasonably in the interest of national security. The Supreme Court has stated that "no governmental interest is more compelling than the security of the Nation," and that the "President has constitutional authority to protect the national security, and that this authority carries with it broad discretion,"[42] which is in line with the utilitarian analysis.

Torture abolitionists might make two arguments against the use of waterboarding even if it is not considered torture. First, an abuse argument: that the necessity argument fails because torture has come to be applied widely.[43] In instances where waterboarding is a legitimate necessity, interrogators may nevertheless not use waterboarding because it would become standard practice when information is needed even at lower levels of urgency.

However, it should not be the case that abuses prevent the proper application. By analogy, there are two types of opioid use: permissible (prescribed) and impermissible (recreational). The impermissible use has not resulted in a regulation stating that all opioid use is impermissible, because there are certain instances where it is necessary. The abuse is what must be condemned—not the proper use. The majority report the court references in *Ireland* addresses this concern, stating that the morality of such a technique would depend in part on "the existence of safeguards against their excessive use."[44] If it is made clear what acts constitute torture and what acts constitute ill-treatment, it can be made clear what safeguards must be in place to protect against excessive use of the latter in the interest of national security.

The necessity defense appears to be valid because the US has continuing national security concerns and the techniques used in the interest of national security actually work. Further, under a utilitarian analysis, which was the ethical perspective adopted by the court in *Israel*, the necessity defense is legitimate. Thus, even if the definition of torture were expanded to include waterboarding, it would be an acceptable interrogation technique for the purpose of national security.

However, the Convention against Torture notes that "no exceptional circumstances whatsoever may be invoked by a State Party to justify acts of torture," which means that the prohibition against torture is absolute, and the necessity defense is invalid.[45] This guidance was offered as a reaction to the post-9/11 CIA interrogation activities, which illustrates an important point: Much of the discussion about the permissibility of torture, the necessity defense, and what constitutes torture came about because of the CIA's reaction to terrorist attacks on American soil. Flimsy laws allowed for workarounds, and only recently has there been a minor victory for the elusive concept of accountability in this context.

In 2017 a settlement was reached in a lawsuit against two individuals who helped develop the CIA's post-9/11 interrogation program. James Mitchell and Bruce Jessen were former psychologists in the United States military's Survival, Evasion, Resistance, and Escape (SERE) program. As such, they trained US troops to resist abusive treatment in violation of the Geneva Conventions in case of capture, using controlled versions of techniques used by authoritarian regimes.[46] In December 2001, months after the 9/11 attacks, the CIA commissioned the psychologists to review the Manchester Manual, which the CIA believed to be an instruction manual for al Qaida operatives on how to resist interrogation.

Mitchell and Jensen provided a report to the CIA that offered ways to defeat such resistance, putting forth the idea that they would be able to design a program that would psychologically destroy detainees and would render them compliant with interrogators' demands. Their report relied on the concept of learned helplessness, defined as the "state of utter passivity prompted by a series of negative events that leads subjects to believe there is nothing they can do to escape their suffering."[47] In practice, the idea was that once detainees were abused enough, they would enter a state of learned helplessness, would no longer resist interrogation, and would offer information that they would not otherwise offer.

The American Civil Liberties Union (ACLU) has stated that this process amounts to an experiment. No studies have been produced to research the concept of learned helplessness, because the study itself would amount to torture, according to psychologist Steven Reisner:

> *Inducing a state of learned helplessness in humans, I think without doubt, would constitute torture—cruel, inhuman, or degrading treatment. Which is the reason why we can't do such experiments, because just envisioning, just actually setting up such an experiment, is a violation of human dignity and a violation of the prohibitions against cruel, inhuman, and degrading treatment.*[48]

Such research has been explicitly banned since The Nuremberg Code was put in place in 1947, which prohibits research on individuals without their informed consent. Indeed, research using prisoners in standard American prisons is largely prohibited in the United States for fear of violating the requirements of informed consent—using prisoners for experimentation in military detention camps—who are even more prone to coercion—would be an even more precarious undertaking. Yet, Mitchell and Jessen reported that for detainee Abu Zubaydah, an interrogator would snap his finger twice and Zubaydah would lie flat on the waterboard. "Our goal was to reach the stage where we have broken any will or ability of subject to resist or deny providing us information (intelligence) to which he had access."[49]

Whether or not it is clear that this constitutes an "experiment," the involvement of Mitchell and Jessen in the interrogation program allowed for the argument to be put forward for the legality of the interrogations, since they were being monitored by health professionals to make sure that they were safe.

In 2015, the ACLU filed suit against the two psychologists on behalf of former US detainees, alleging that they "designed, implemented, and personally administered an experimental torture program for the [CIA]."[50] In 2017, the case settled. The American Psychological Association (APA) released a statement saying that "this does not absolve [the psychologists] of responsibility for violating the ethics of their profession."[51] The situation precipitated an amendment to the APA's Code of Ethics; it now states the following:

> *Torture in any form, at any time, in any place, and for any reason, is unethical for psychologists and wholly inconsistent with membership in the American Psychological Association. No exceptional circumstances whatsoever, whether a state of war or a threat or war, internal political instability or any other public emergency, legal compulsion or organizational demand, may be invoked as a justification for torture. There is no defense to torture under the Ethical Principles of Psychologists and Code of Conduct (2002, as amended 2010). The APA Ethics Committee will not accept any defense to torture in its adjudication of ethics complaints.*[52]

While APA's policy now prohibits psychologists from participating in national security interrogations at detention sites operating in violation of US or international law, this does not amount to an adjudication on the merits in a challenge to post-9/11 counterterrorism interrogation policies and practices.

Further, at the time, the "enhanced interrogation techniques" were not clearly illegal, particularly since in a 2002 memo, President Bush stated that the Geneva Conventions' protections do not apply to al Qaida and Taliban detainees, because, in part, al Qaeda is not a High Contracting Party to Geneva.[53] Only after the interrogation practices came to light was there an unequivocal ban put in place, with a ban on waterboarding specifically being enacted in January 2009 by Executive Order 13491 under President Obama.[54] This case illustrates the importance of clarity in US policies in order to combat impunity.

Even if the validity of the necessity defense is not agreed upon within the US, or if it is unclear whether conditioning detainees to learned helplessness is a violation of Geneva despite al Qaeda not being a High Contracting Party, one way to move forward is to make stipulations. Where there is vagueness, there is impunity. To protect against impunity in the context of waterboarding, we may stipulate either of the following: 1) Whether or not waterboarding is torture, we accept that waterboarding is permissible, but the US does not engage in any other forms of torture; or 2) Waterboarding is torture even though linguistic acrobatics may result in plausible actual cause arguments to the contrary, and therefore the US does not permit or implement waterboarding techniques. Both of these stipulations make it clear what the US position is, thus those who violate the policy will be held accountable. Implementing a clear policy would make it apparent when that policy is violated, and interrogators would no longer be able to "cross the line" with impunity, arguing that no one has agreed where the line actually is.

D. The morality of using information gathered as a result of morally impermissible actions

While it may be stipulated that the US does not permit waterboarding, and while those who impermissibly use waterboarding in interrogations would thus more readily be held accountable, there remains the question of whether it is permissible to use information gathered during illegal interrogations. Ideally, where clear laws are in place, no one would violate them. In reality, there is a risk that such laws will be violated—intentionally or as a result of miscommunication/misunderstanding; there is also the risk that situations will arise that the law does not precisely address, and only after actions are taken are those actions deemed to be violations of international law and human rights. Given the risk of these situations occurring, it is important to stipulate also what the US policy is regarding whether or not information gained through illegal interrogations (whether those interrogations were illegal at the time or found to have been illegal after the fact) is usable.

Similar dilemmas have arisen in the past. In 1937, Unit 731 in China was created with the intention to benefit Japanese soldiers. Scientists had hoped to understand how the body fights diseases, and how humans can survive hunger and thirst. Initially, consenting volunteers were used as research participants. Soon, however, the types of experiments changed dramatically. Despite the ban on the use of biochemical weapons in warfare, the Japanese wanted to be prepared for the use of biological and chemical weapons during the war.[55] It was impossible to find willing research participants for these types of experiments, however. Thus, Unit 731 began using prisoners of war— largely Chinese and Russians, as well as Mongolians and Koreans—to conduct research on biochemical agents.

It is widely known that the Nazis conducted medical experiments on prisoners in concentration camps during World War II, but Unit 731's atrocities have largely been kept quiet. As were the medical experiments conducted in concentration camps, the experiments conducted by Japanese scientists were gruesome—and left no survivors. Victims would be infected with different diseases, and researchers would perform vivisections to see how the body responded to the disease. The vivisections were performed on live victims—without anesthesia, for fear that it would have an effect on the results—so that researchers could observe the body's response before organs began their process of decay after death.[56] A medical assistant in a Japanese Army unit in China during this time spoke with the *New York Times* in 1995 to detail what it was like to carry out such an experiment: "I cut him open from the chest to the stomach, and he screamed terribly, and his face was all twisted in agony. He made this unimaginable sound, he was screaming so horribly. But then finally he stopped."[57] The prisoner had been infected with the Bubonic plague in order to develop plague bombs for use in World War II.

In some instances, researchers infected male prisoners with syphilis and ordered them to rape female prisoners. Females who were involuntarily impregnated would then become the subject of further experimentation and vivisection to see how syphilis affected the mother and the fetus. Yoshimura Hisato, a Unit 731 researcher, took particular interest in studying the effects of freezing on human limbs. He would hold prisoners' limbs in tubs of ice water until the limb had frozen completely.[58] He would then study the effects of frostbite, as well as different methods for rapid rewarming.

These experiments are incontrovertibly torturous, even though they were carried out in the name of science rather than for the purpose of torture itself. However, the true ethical question in this instance is not whether the experiments were unethical as torture, but what should have been done with the results of such experiments. Is it ethical to use the data gathered under such circumstances, if such data is indeed useful to the medical community? There are a few options: 1) We could destroy the data or simply not use them, because using information gathered by means of torture is unethical; 2) We could use the data if they are in our possession, because if we didn't, then the torture would have been for nothing; 3) We could trade impunity for the data because the data are critical to advancements in medical knowledge. Option 3, while it may seem absurd, is the reality of what happened after Unit 731 was closed at the end of World War II.

The decision to not hold any of the Japanese scientists accountable for committing these atrocities so that we could obtain their data has been criticized as trading justice for science.

Those in favor of this decision would argue that the data were comprehensive, could not otherwise have been obtained, and form the foundation for critical medical knowledge that we would not otherwise have today. While impunity is a hard pill to swallow, it is outweighed by the broad benefit that the data confer upon us.

Opponents of the decision would argue that using information obtained through torture is tantamount to condoning torture, and trading impunity for such information inflicts further harm because there will never be justice for the victims of the Unit 731 experiments. They were tortured, and their torturers walked free because the result of their torture was useful.

There is no consensus on what should have been done with the data gathered by Unit 731 scientists, but the conversation surrounding what was in fact done in the aftermath can serve as a guide for analyzing whether the information gathered through post-9/11 illegal interrogations is usable. If we were to follow precedent, we would look at the Unit 731 case and determine that if the information is valuable enough it may be used, even if that results in impunity for wrongdoers. Because this is a simplified takeaway from the Unit 731 case, we must stipulate the US policy.

For example, we would first say that it is the policy of the United States to not engage in torture. Then we would address the reality that not everyone will adhere to this policy; we could state that if an interrogator illegally tortures a prisoner, and as a result gains valuable information, we will/will not use that information to further our cause. Then we must address the fact that even if we use the information illegally obtained, the perpetrator will be held accountable for his illegal actions.

The overarching ethical question that arose from the Unit 731 case was not necessarily about what to do with the information gathered, but about the impunity that was bestowed upon the perpetrators. In post-9/11 America, the situation is somewhat different. Information would not necessarily be withheld as a bargaining chip as it was when the Japanese scientists were the ones who had gathered the information for themselves, because the interrogator in a post-9/11 case would already be working for the United States. However, we still must make clear that there will be no impunity for those who violate US policy. If this were not stated, the US policy would be weak. It would be possible for interrogators to illegally torture prisoners, obtain information for the United

States, and ask for impunity because of the value of the information gathered. This would not act as a deterrent for future interrogators, who might believe that even if they violate policy, there will be no consequences. It is necessary to analyze the ethical questions that arose from the case of Unit 731 in order to formulate acceptable post-9/11 information gathering policies.

E. Policy Considerations

Even if there were a justifiable reason for waterboarding (i.e., the necessity defense), the information gained may not outweigh the information lost when nations are no longer willing to share intelligence with the US because we are seen as a nation that tortures.[59] While it is important to resolve issues of morality and legality domestically, it is equally important to consider how those resolutions are communicated to and understood by the international community. Whether or not waterboarding legally fits the definition of torture is not the driving factor when considering diplomatic relations. It would be difficult to quantify both the amount of information gained as a result of post-9/11 waterboarding interrogations, and the amount of information lost if nations were to withhold intelligence—which cuts against the necessity defense.

To minimize the risk the potential loss of key information from other nations, it may be argued that the US must stipulate that waterboarding is not permissible as a policy matter, whether or not it is regarded as torture. However, it may be that the intelligence lost post-9/11 was because nations saw no clear statement that waterboarding is not considered torture, and deduced in the absence of such a declaration that because the US engaged in waterboarding, we are a nation that engages in torture. Therefore, it would likely be sufficient to clarify that the US is not a nation that tortures, and approves waterboarding as an interrogation technique because it does not regard waterboarding as torture. In either case, clarity is key.

[4]

Conclusion

WATERBOARDING DOES NOT fit the legal definitions of mental or physical torture. Despite this, it is necessary to analyze the morality of waterboarding. I have illustrated how a deontologist and utilitarian would analyze the validity of the necessity defense, and proposed a practical solution to the debate given the need for clarity to protect against impunity. Finally, I concluded that even if waterboarding is legally not torture and is morally permissible in certain situations, it may nevertheless be necessary to stipulate that waterboarding is impermissible as a policy matter from an informational cost-benefit perspective.

ABOUT THE AUTHOR

Kaitlin Puccio is an award-winning writer, filmmaker, lawyer, and business owner. She was previously a Fellow at the Institute of International Economic Law, and a ghostwriter for a member of President Obama's Advisory Council on Financial Capability. She is also a member of Meridian International Center and Global Women's Innovation Network in Washington, D.C. Her writing has been translated into several languages, including French, Italian, Finnish, Portuguese, Estonian, and Spanish. She holds a BA in philosophy from New York University, a JD from Georgetown Law, and an MS in bioethics from Columbia University.

ABOUT KAYE LABS

Kaye Labs is the research and consulting side of the Celia Kaye brand that focuses on the intersection of bioethics and law.

NOTES

[1] UN General Assembly, *Convention Against Torture and Other Cruel, Inhuman or Degrading Treatment or Punishment*, Art. 1 10 December 1984, United Nations, Treaty Series, vol. 1465, p. 85.]

[2] UN General Assembly, *Rome Statute of the International Criminal Court (last amended 2010)*, 17 July 1998, ISBN No. 92-9227-227-6.

[3] 18 U.S. Code § 2441

[4] *See also* Prosecutor v. Kunarac, IT-96-23, stating that three elements of the definition of torture in the Torture Convention are uncontested and accepted as representing the status of customary international law: (i) Torture consists of the infliction, by act or omission, of severe pain or suffering, whether physical or mental. (ii) This act or omission must be intentional. (iii) The act must be instrumental to another purpose, in the sense that the infliction of pain must be aimed at reaching a certain goal.

[5] Fact-Check: Could The Next President Bring Back Waterboarding? NPR, February 13, 2016.

[6] Coral Dando, I specialise in the psychology of torture, so I know the truth behind Trump's claims that waterboarding works, *The Independent*, January 26, 2017.

[7] Jacobs, "Documenting the Neurobiology of Psychological Torture," 165–67.

[8] *The Defense Department Working Group Report on Detainee Interrogations in the Global War on Terrorism: Assessment of Legal, Historical, Policy, and Operational Considerations*, April 4, 2003, p. 4.

[9] Id. at 16.

[10] Id.

[11] Id. at 14-16.

[12] There are those who have stated that waterboarding is torture after having voluntarily subjected themselves to waterboarding experiments. Given that here is no agreed upon definition of torture, it is difficult to discern which definition of torture to which the subjects are referring. Further, "torture" has colloquial meaning, which may take into account an individual's subjective experience more so than the legal definition. Because of these nuances, a pronouncement that something is (and/or feels like) torture would need to be analyzed in greater detail than space allows here.

[13] Brook, Timothy, et al. *Death by a Thousand Cuts.* Harvard University Press, 2008.

[14] It is debatable whether the torture techniques used during the Spanish Inquisition, in reality, were a means to an end, or the end itself. The confessions extracted via torture were often names of other people who would then be subjected to their own torture, indicating that torture was used more as a means to employ more torture. The history of the Spanish Inquisition and the psychology of Tomás de Torquemada, the Grand Inquisitor, are outside the scope of this writing, but are worth considering when analyzing the purpose of torture as an interrogation technique.

[15] Egypt: Torture Epidemic May Be Crime Against Humanity, Human Rights Watch, September 6, 2017.

[16] UN General Assembly, *Convention Against Torture and Other Cruel, Inhuman or Degrading Treatment or Punishment*, Art. 1 10 December 1984, United Nations, Treaty Series, vol. 1465, p. 85.

[17] *See* Hudgens v. Prosper, Inc., 2011 WL8181959 (Utah Dist.Ct.), where an employee brought a tort claim arising out of a waterboarding incident. Note that the supervisor in this case was presumably not trained in waterboarding technique, whereas national security agents who apply the technique would be trained to apply the technique properly.

[18] Black's Law Dictionary, "tort"

[19] Black's Law Dictionary, "willful tort"

[20] *See* Ryan v. New York Central R.R., 35 N.Y. 210, 1866 N.Y. 86.

[21] Verified via a conversation with William Lietzau, former Deputy Assistant Secretary of Defense for Rule of Law and Detainee Policy at the U.S. Department of Defense.

[22] Garvin, Glenn, *Miami Herald*: "Ugly Truth: Sometimes, Torture Works," May 6, 2013.

[23] *See generally* Rand Corporation, "Connecting the Dots" in Intelligence: Detecting Terrorist Threats in the Out-of-the-Ordinary. Also note that "Does torture work?" may also refer to whether torture works as a deterrent. Like those during the Spanish Inquisition who made confessions even before being strapped to the rack due to the mere possibility of their own shoulders being stretched, the threat of waterboarding may be enough to extract information, as long as the subject knows that it is a real possibility. In the interest of space, I will leave this analysis to a later date.

[24] *Committee Study of the Central Intelligence Agency's Detention and Interrogation Program*, Senate Select Committee on Intelligence, Redacted Executive Summary released December 9, 2014.

[25] CIA Oversight Report, Congressional Record, daily edition, vol. 160, no. 149 (December 9, 2014), pp. S6405-S6444.

[26] US v. Oakland Cannabis Buyers' Co-op, 532 U.S. 483, 490 (2001).

[27] Ireland v. United Kingdom, *1976 Y.B. Eur. Conv. on Hum. Rts.*

[28] Id. at 5.

[29] Id. at 24.

[30] *Report of the Enquiry into Allegations Against the Security Forces of Physical Brutality in Northern Ireland Arising Out of Events on the 9th August, 1971*, CMD. No. 4-823, at iii, (Gr. Britain 1971).

[31] Id. at 13.

[32] *Report of the Committee of Privy Counsellors Appointed to Consider Authorized Procedures for the Interrogation of Persons Suspected of Terrorism*, CMD. No. 4901, at v, (Gr. Britain 1972). [hereinafter cited as Parker Report].

[33] Donahue, Deirdre, *Human Rights in Northern Ireland: Ireland v. the United Kingdom*, Boston College International and Comparative Law Review, Vol. 3, August 1, 1980.

[34] Parker Report at 7.

[35] Public Committee Against Torture in Israel v. Israel, H.C. 5100/94 (Isr. S. Ct. 1999).

[36] Id. at 30.

[37] Hayden, Michael, *The Hill*: Americans Are Safer From Terrorists But New Threats Are Arising, October 15, 2018.

[38] Garamone, Jim, U.S. Department of Defense, "Cyber Tops List of Threats to U.S., Director of National Intelligence Says," February 13, 2018.

[39] Driver, Julia, *The Stanford Encyclopedia of Philosophy,* "The History of Utilitarianism," (Winter 2014 Edition), Edward N. Zalta (ed.).

[40] Alexander, Larry and Moore, Michael, *The Stanford Encyclopedia of Philosophy*, "Deontological Ethics," (Winter 2016 Edition), Edward N. Zalta (ed.).

[41] I will not address the ticking time bomb scenario closely in this writing, though it is a worthwhile discussion. Here, I will assume that long-term and imminent life-saving are morally equal, though I recognize that there are arguments that ticking time bomb scenarios only extend to imminent life-saving. In this writing, I assume that the necessity defense is not limited to ticking time bomb scenarios, as I interpret the above courts' decisions as having used such a scenario as a point of illustration, not of limitation.

[42] Hamdi v. Rumsfeld, 124 S.Ct. 2633, 2675 (2004). *See also Haig v. Agee*, 101 S.Ct. 2766 (1981).

[43] *See The Economist*, "Torture: Ends, Means and Barbarity," January 9, 2003.

[44] Donahue, Deirdre, *Boston College International and Comparative Law Review*, "Human Rights in Northern Ireland: Ireland v. the United Kingdom," Vol. 3, August 1, 1980.

[45] Convention against Torture, art. 2(2); UN Committee Against Torture, General Comment 2, CAT/C/GC/2 (2008).

[46] Id.

[47] Yachot, Noa, "Out of the Darkness," ACLU, October 13, 2015.

[48] Id.

[49] Id.

[50] *Salim v. Mitchell*, 183 F. Supp. 3d 1121, (E.D. Wash. 2016).

[51] "APA Reaction to Settlement of Torture Case Against Psychologists Mitchell, Jessen," APA, August 17, 2017.

[52] APA Ethics Committee Statement – No Defense to Torture, June, 2009 (as amended November 2015).

[53] Derek Jinks and David Sloss, Is the President Bound by the Geneva Conventions, 90 Cornell L. Rev. 97 (2004).

[54] Federal Register (January 27, 2009), v.74 n.16, p.4893-4896.

[55] Keiichi, Tsuneishi, "Unit 731 and the Japanese Imperial Army's Biological Warfare Program," *The Asia-Pacific Journal*, Volume 3, Issue 11, November 24, 2005.

[56] Kristof, Nicholas D., "Unmasking Horror – A Special Report; Japan Confronting Gruesome War Atrocity, *The New York Times*, March 17, 1995.

[57] Id.

[58] Id.; Tsuchiya Takashi, Osaka City University, "Self Determination by Imperial Japanese Doctors: Did They Freely Decide to Perform Deadly Experiments?", UNESCO-Kumamoto University Bioethics Roundtable, December 16, 2007.

[59] This concern was expressed during a conversation with William Lietzau, former Deputy Assistant Secretary of Defense for Rule of Law and Detainee Policy at the U.S. Department of Defense.

www.ingramcontent.com/pod-product-compliance
Lightning Source LLC
Chambersburg PA
CBHW030458010526
44118CB00011B/995